# Job Aids for Everyone

## A Step-by-Step Guide to Creating Job and Task Aids

**Charlotte Long**

**HRD Press, Inc. • Amherst • Massachusetts**

Published by:   HRD Press
                22 Amherst Road
                Amherst, MA 01002
                (800) 822-2801
                (413) 253-3490 fax
                http://www.hrdpress.com

ISBN 0-087425-791-3

Cover Design by Eileen Klockars
Editorial Services by Sally Farnham
Production Services by Anctil Virtual Office

# Table of Contents

# Introduction

Are you frustrated by learning that does not transfer to the workplace?

Are you tired of explaining things over and over?

Do you feel that sometimes training is overkill for a performance problem?

Then you need to know about creating **Job Aids for Everyone.**

Job aids are also called performance support tools and task aids. They help the worker take the correct or best action and can take many forms.

| **Which of the following do you think are job aids?** | |
| --- | --- |
| | Chocolate Chip Cookie Recipe |
| | Push/Pull Door Signs |
| | Computer Software Help Screens |
| | Toy Assembly Instructions |
| | ATM Screen Directions |
| | Traffic Lights |
| | Handwritten Sticky Notes |

**Turn the page to check your answers.**

If you picked all of them, you are right! Each one helps the worker take the correct or best action.

What is a job aid you use? _____

Do you see any value in job aids?_____

If you said yes, you have a high probability of creating good job aids after reading this book.

If you said no, you might have difficulty creating effective job aids at the conclusion of study. Please continue though; you might like what you see.

## Assumptions

**To best use the information in this book, it is assumed that you can do the following:**

1. Develop an effective plan for gathering task data.
   *A task is a discrete work activity with a distinct beginning and ending.*

> **Throughout this book, we will use the term *job aid* instead of task aid or performance support tool; however, keep in mind that a single job aid can address only a discrete work activity, not all aspects of the larger job.**

2. Individually or with others gather data on a task.
3. Using data, describe the detailed behaviors of the task.
4. Validate performance problems at the task level.
   *A performance problem is the gap between what is happening and what should be happening.*

If you lack any of these skills, you might have difficulty with the information in this book. You will need to acquire these skills to create effective job aids.

These skills allow you to establish the foundations of an effective job aid as shown below:

   • Clearly define the target workers who will be using your job aid.

> **This is critical! You will refer to this throughout the creation of the job aid since an effective job aid *must* be based on the target workers' perspective, knowledge, skills, and environment.**

   • Identify the performance gap.
   • Determine whether a job aid might eliminate or reduce the performance gap.
   • Describe the steps to correctly complete the task.

You will need to refer back to these foundations throughout the process of creating a job aid.

When you complete this book, you will be able to design effective job aids using the process shown below:

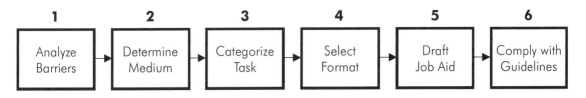

## Practice Job Aid

Throughout this self-study book, you will be asked to create your own job aid. This exercise is extremely important. Actually creating a job aid is more difficult than it might seem. Please take the time to create your practice job aid.

Now remove or copy the **Practice Job Aid Worksheet** in Appendix A on pages 63–71 and follow these instructions:

1. Select a very *simple* task that you can do very well. Examples of possible tasks are listed below:
   - Making iced tea
   - Starting a lawn mower
   - Microwaving popcorn
   - Sending a fax

   > **NOTE: Job aids are NOT appropriate if the task must be completed very quickly. It is best to memorize emergency tasks.**

2. When you have selected your topic, write your selected task at the top of the **Practice Job Aid Worksheet**.
3. Clearly define the target workers who will be using your job aid.
4. When done, return to the book to learn how to analyze barriers.

**Ready? Go to the next page for Phase 1—Analyze Barriers.**

# Phase 1—Analyze Barriers

The first phase is to analyze barriers that would bar the use of a job aid.

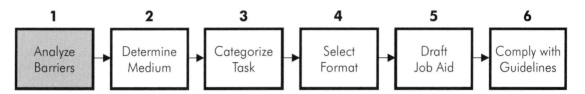

Below is a flowchart that shows the process for completing Phase 1—Analyze Barriers.

## Figure 1: Analyze Barriers

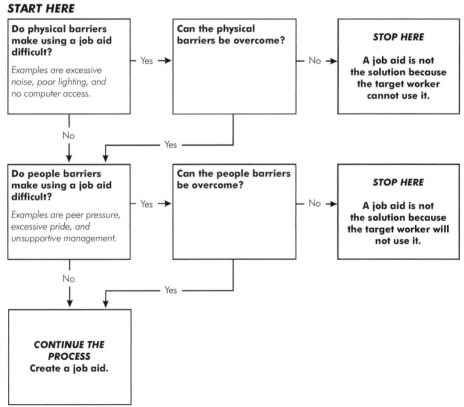

## Case Example for Phase 1—Analyze Barriers

*Target Workers:* All sales representatives.

*Task:* The sales representatives need a summary of the key features of your company's new product so they can appear knowledgeable when speaking with a client.

*1. Analyze Barriers:*

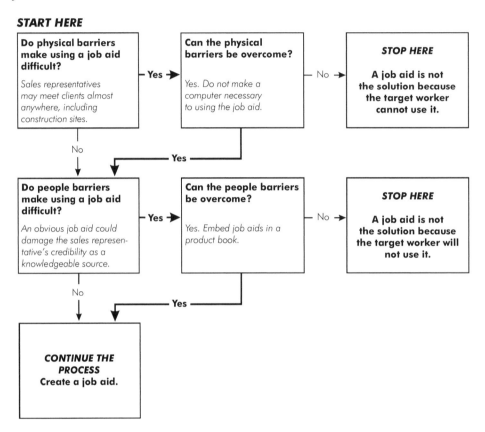

**Go to the next page for Practice 1 for Phase 1—Analyze Barriers.**

## Practice 1 for Phase 1—Analyze Barriers

Referring to Figure 1: Analyze Barriers analyze the barriers for the situation below by filling in the flowchart that follows.

*Target Workers:* Customer Service Representatives (CSRs)

*Validated Performance Problem at the Task Level:* CSRs are not posting complaints. CSRs should post complaints in a mainframe database accessed through Windows-based computer.

---

### How to Use a Flowchart
1. Start at the first box.
2. Answer the question or complete the activity in the box.
3. Follow the directional arrow for your answer to the next box.
4. Repeat steps 2 and 3 above until you reach an ending box.
*Idea:* You may want to trace your path with a yellow highlighter.

---

**START HERE**

| Do physical barriers make using a job aid difficult? | →Yes→ | Can the physical barriers be overcome? | →No→ | **STOP HERE** A job aid is not the solution because the target worker cannot use it. |

No ↓ (from first box) / Yes → (from "Can the physical barriers be overcome?")

| Do people barriers make using a job aid difficult? | →Yes→ | Can the people barriers be overcome? | →No→ | **STOP HERE** A job aid is not the solution because the target worker will not use it. |

No ↓ (from "Do people barriers") / Yes → (from "Can the people barriers be overcome?")

| **CONTINUE THE PROCESS** Create a job aid. |

---

**When you're ready, go to the next page for the answer key.**

## Answer Key for Practice 1 for Phase 1—Analyze Barriers

Below are the answers for Practice 1. Check all the items you included in your answer and score yourself.

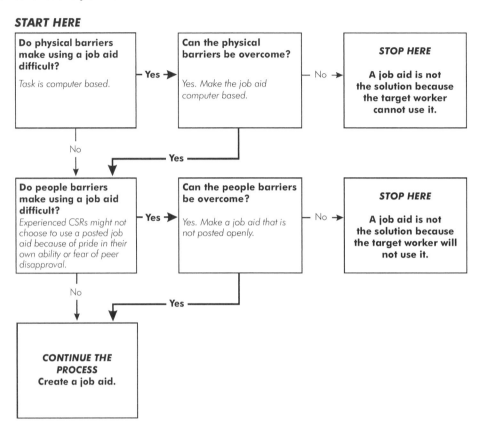

If your answer matches the answer key, great job! You understand how to analyze barriers. You may skip Practice 2 and go directly to the **Practice Job Aid** and analyze the barriers for your job aid. When you are done, return to the book to learn how to determine the best medium for a job aid.

If you missed one step, good work. Remember that analyzing barriers thoroughly is critical to the ultimate success of a job aid. Try Practice 2 on the next page.

If your answer does not match the answer key, you are having difficulty with this important step. You should review the course material before proceeding to Practice 2. Do not be discouraged; it can take a while to get the hang of it.

**Go to the next page for Practice 2 for Phase 1—Analyze Barriers.**

## Practice 2 for Phase 1—Analyze Barriers

Referring to Figure 1: Analyze Barriers analyze the barriers for the situation below by filling out the flowchart that follows.

*Target Workers:* Middle managers, regardless of managerial experience

*Validated Performance Problem at the Task Level:* Managers do not consistently report employees' overtime to the Human Resources database.

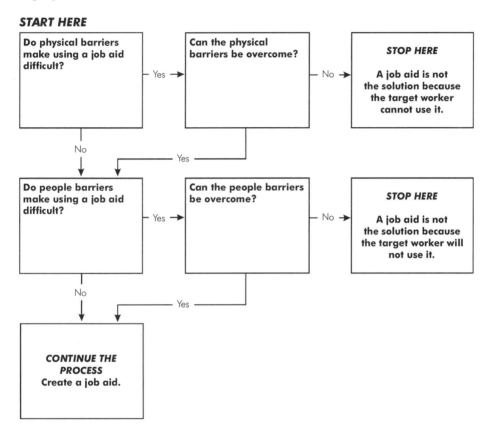

**When you're ready, go to the next page for the answer key.**

## Answer Key for Practice 2 for Phase 1—Analyze Barriers

Below are the answers for Practice 2. Check all the items you included in your answer and score yourself.

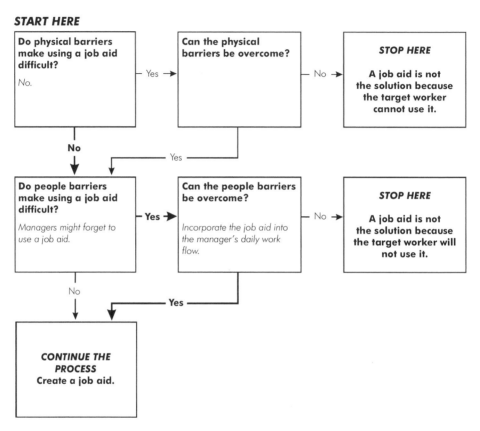

If your answer matches the answer key, great job! You understand how to analyze barriers.

If you missed one step, good work. Remember that analyzing barriers thoroughly is critical to the ultimate success of a job aid.

If your answer does not match the answer key, you are having difficulty with this important step. You should review the course material before proceeding. Keep trying; you can do this.

**Go to the next page to complete
Phase 1—Analyze Barriers for your *Practice Job Aid Worksheet.***

## Practice Job Aid

Go to your **Practice Job Aid Worksheet** on page 66 and analyze the barriers to using your job aid. Think carefully. This is a critical step.

When completed, return to the book to learn how to determine the best medium for a job aid.

**You are doing great!**
**Now it's time to move on to Phase 2—Determine Medium.**

# Phase 2—Determine Medium

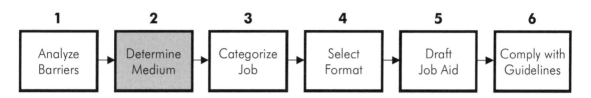

In determining the correct medium for the job aid, compare your completed barrier analysis with the various media.

**Go to the next page for Table 2: Media Advantages and Disadvantages.**

### Table 2.1: Media Advantages and Disadvantages with Examples

| Medium | Advantages | Disadvantages | Examples |
|---|---|---|---|
| Computer-Based | Effective for computer-related jobs<br><br>Always in the same place<br><br>Can be permanent<br><br>Can often be printed<br><br>Appeals to computer-literate workers only<br><br>Current version available | Dependent on computer and proper connectivity<br><br>If printing required, requires each worker to have reasonable access to a good printer<br><br>Might require Information Technology personnel to implement and update<br><br>May require all workers to have updated software<br><br>Can be difficult for worker to easily locate | Expert systems<br><br>Help screens<br><br>Online procedures |
| Hard-Copy | Effective when job aid needs to be visible constantly<br><br>Can take many forms such as sticky notes, laminated cards, wall charts, etc.<br><br>Easier to read than on screen<br><br>Can easily be portable<br><br>Workers can customize by making notes on aid | Easy to misplace<br><br>Difficult to update<br><br>Wears out with use<br><br>May become illegible due to repeated photocopying | Reference page<br><br>Wallet help cards<br><br>Wall chart<br><br>Worksheet |
| Integrated<br>*Job aid is part of a larger hard-copy or computer-based documentation.* | Effective when job aid is to be hidden until needed<br><br>Automatically presented to the worker when appropriate | Can be easily accessed only while performing the larger job process. | Pop-up help on computer<br><br>Glued or permanently attached to equipment |
| Stand-Alone | Effective when job is not part of a larger job or is an easily recognized common element in many jobs | Worker might not refer to the job aid when appropriate<br><br>Easy to misplace | Printed help screens<br><br>Reference book or manual |

**Go to the next page for a Case Example for Phase 2—Determine Medium.**

Referring to Table 2.1: Media Advantages and Disadvantages with Examples, study the case example below.

## Case Example for Phase 2—Determine Medium

*Target Workers:* New trainers

*Validated Performance Problem at the Task Level:* New trainers do not know how to ensure proper display of a video when others provide the VCR and monitor.

*Phase 1. Analyze Barriers*

Physical Barriers? The trainer will not have easy access to a computer and may have already brought a large quantity of paper. These barriers can be overcome.

People Barriers? There should be no people barriers because the trainers will practice the operation before the students arrive. If the trainer needs a refresher using the VCR in front of the class, the barrier can be overcome.

*Phase 2. Analyze the Media:* A computer-based job aid is inappropriate because the trainers might not have access to a computer. A hard-copy job aid would be preferable since the task steps are stable. Since a hard-copy can be misplaced, it should catch the eye. The effective trainer will want to complete this task successfully in front of a class; therefore, the disadvantage of a stand-alone job aid (that is, worker might not refer to the job aid when appropriate) does not apply in this situation.

### Table 2.2: Instructions for Determining the Medium

| IF | AND | THEN |
|---|---|---|
| Computer-based | Integrated | Select computer-based integrated medium |
| | Stand-alone | Select computer-based stand-alone medium |
| Hard-copy | Integrated | Select hard-copy integrated medium |
| | Stand-alone | Select hard-copy stand-alone medium |

*Determine Medium:* The job aid should be a stand-alone, hard-copy medium. Consider using a color laminated 8½" × 11" sheet for durability and visibility.

**Go to the next page for Practice 1 for Phase 2—Determine Medium.**

## Practice 1 for Phase 2—Determine Medium

Referring to Table 2.1: Media Advantages and Disadvantages with Examples, and Table 2.2: Instructions for Determining the Medium, determine the correct medium for the performance issue below.

*Target Workers:* Customer Service Representatives (CSRs)

*Validated Performance Problem at the Task Level:* CSRs are not posting complaints within the established deadlines. Complaints are posted in a mainframe database accessed through Windows-based computers.

*Analyze Barriers:* There are no physical barriers. There are people barriers: Experienced CSRs might not use a posted job aid because of pride in their own ability or fear of peer disapproval.

*Determine Medium:*

| Medium | Your Decision |
|---|---|
| Computer-based? | |
| Hard-copy? | |
| Integrated? | |
| Stand-alone? | |
| **Your Media Decision** | |

**When you're ready, go to the next page for the answer key.**

# Answer Key for Practice 1 for Phase 2—Determine Medium

Below are the answers for Practice 1. Check all the items you included in your answer and score yourself.

| Medium | Decision | Give yourself one point for each match. |
|---|---|---|
| Computer-based? | Yes. The job is computer-related. Since late-posted complaints adversely affect the company profits, the cost of Information Technology support is justified. | |
| Hard-copy? | No. This job is triggered by the passage of time. The worker might not know when to use the job aid. | |
| Integrated? | Yes. It is important to automatically present the job aid to the worker when it is appropriate. | |
| Stand-alone? | No. Posting complaints is part of a long-term process. In addition, the major problem is that the workers are not posting complaints within deadlines. | |
| Media Decision | Computer-based and Integrated | |
| | **YOUR SCORE** | |

If you made the correct media decision with a score of 4 or 5, great job! You have successfully completed a media analysis. You may skip Practice 2 for Phase 2 and go directly to the **Practice Job Aid Worksheet** and determine the correct medium for your job aid.

If you made the correct media decision with a score of 1, 2, or 3, you are on the right track. Remember: A well thought out media analysis immensely increases your odds of making a correct media decision. Go to Practice 2 for Phase 2 on the next page.

If you made an incorrect media decision, review the course material before proceeding to Practice 2 for Phase 2. A media decision can be complicated; have patience with yourself.

**Go to the next page for Practice 2 for Phase 2—Determine Medium.**

## Practice 2 for Phase 2—Determine Medium

Referring to Table 2.1: Media Advantages and Disadvantages with Examples Table 2.2: Instructions for Determining the Medium and the Practice 1 for Phase 2 answer key, determine the best media for the performance issue below.

*Target Workers:* All middle managers

*Validated Performance Problem at the Task Level:* Middle managers do not consistently report their employees' overtime

*Phase 1. Analyze Barriers:* There are no physical barriers. There are people barriers: The manager might forget to enter the overtime data on time. This can be overcome.

*Phase 2. Determine Medium:*

| Medium | Your Decision |
|---|---|
| Computer-based? | |
| Hard-copy? | |
| Integrated? | |
| Stand-alone? | |
| **Your Media Decision** | |

**When you're ready, go to the next page for the answer key.**

## Answer Key for Practice 2 for Phase 2—Determine Medium

Below are the answers for Practice 2. Check all the items you included in your answer and score yourself.

| Medium | Decision | Give yourself one point for each match. |
|---|---|---|
| Computer-based? | Yes. This job requires using a computer to access the Human Resources database. | |
| Hard-copy? | No. Easy to misplace. | |
| Integrated? | Yes. Reminder can be automatically presented to the manager when appropriate. | |
| Stand-alone? | No. The manager might not refer to the job aid when appropriate. | |
| Media Decision | Computer-based and Integrated | |
| | YOUR SCORE | |

If you made the correct media decision with a score of 4, you will probably have no difficulty in conducting a media analysis.

If you made the correct media decision with a score of 1, 2, or 3, you are on the right track. Since media analysis is so important, you might want to review the previous material before proceeding to the **Practice Job Aid Worksheet.**

If you made an incorrect media decision, please review the course material before proceeding.

## Practice Job Aid

Now it's your turn to determine the correct media for your practice job aid topic.

Go to your **Practice Job Aid Worksheet** on page 67 and complete Phase 2—Determine Medium.

When done, return to the book to find out how to categorize a task.

**Go to the next page for Phase 3—Categorize Task.**

# Phase 3—Categorize Task

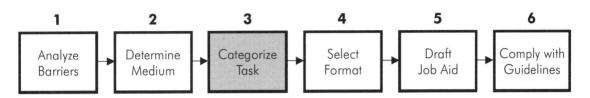

| 1 | 2 | 3 | 4 | 5 | 6 |
|---|---|---|---|---|---|
| Analyze Barriers | Determine Medium | Categorize Task | Select Format | Draft Job Aid | Comply with Guidelines |

To categorize a task, you need to determine whether the task behavior involves sequential steps and/or decision-making behavior.

### Table 3: Categorize Task

| IF . . . | AND . . . | THEN the task category is: |
|----------|-----------|----------------------------|
| The task includes predetermined sequential steps | No decision making | Sequence only<br>*Worker is given the next step.* |
| The task involves making decisions | No predetermined sequential steps | Decision Making only<br>*Worker chooses the next step.* |
| The task involves predetermined sequential steps | Decision making after sequential steps | Decision Making within a Sequence |
| The task involves initial decision making | Predetermined sequential steps after decision making | Initial Decision Making leading to alternate Sequences |

**Go to the next page for a Case Example for Phase 3—Categorize Task.**

## Case Example for Phase 3—Categorize Task

Referring to Table 3: Categorize Task, study the case example below.

*Target Workers:* All employees

*Validated Performance Problem at the Task Level:* Employees do not know how to use Easy Call, the company-approved vendor to host teleconference calls of six or more participants.

*Phase 1. Analyze barriers:*

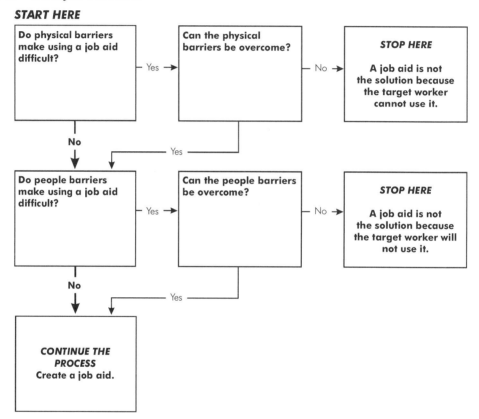

**Continued on the next page.**

## Case Example for Phase 3—Categorize Task *(continued)*

*Phase 2.    Determine medium*

| Medium | Your Decision |
|---|---|
| Computer-based? | No. It might be difficult for worker to easily locate job aid. In addition, the activity itself is not computer-related. The calls may also be made from a remote location. |
| Hard-copy? | Yes. It can be posted or carried with the worker for use at any location or time. |
| Integrated? | No. A teleconference might be necessary at any time on any subject. It would be impossible to integrate it. |
| Stand-alone? | Yes. The worker can refer to the job aid when it is appropriate. |
| **Your Media Decision** | Create a stand-alone, hard-copy job aid. |

*Phase 3.    Categorize Task:*

Task activities:

- Call 1-888-555-5555 to get your Dial-In Number, Conference Code, and Leader Personal Identification Number (PIN).
- Give your Dial-In Number and Conference Code to your participants along with the date and time of the conference call.
- At the time of the teleconference, dial your Dial-In Number.
- Enter your Conference Code when asked.
- When prompted, press * to identify yourself as the call leader, then enter your Leader PIN.
- If you want to record your conference, press *8 to begin recording and *9 to stop.

**Continued on the next page.**

## Case Example for Phase 3—Categorize Task *(concluded)*

| Task Activities Summary | Task Category |
|---|---|
| Five Sequence activities | Sequence |
| One Decision Making activity (If you want to record . . .) | Decision Making |

**Go to the next page for Practice 1 for Phase 3—Categorize Task.**

# Practice 1 for Phase 3—Categorize Task

Referring to Table 3: Categorize Task and the case example, complete the task analysis for the task below.

*Target Workers:* All receptionists

*Proper Task Performance:* When someone enters the office area, the receptionist is expected to do the following:

- Smile

- Immediately make eye contact with the guest

- Immediately acknowledge the guest's presence

- Decide whether to discontinue working on current activity or to explain to the guest why and how long he or she will have to wait

- If decision is to discontinue current activity, focus totally on the guest

- Determine a response that is correct and satisfies the customer

| Task Activities Summary | Task Category |
|---|---|
| (Group together like items in order) | |
| | |
| | |
| | |

**When you're ready, go to the next page for the answer key.**

# Answer Key for Practice 1 for Phase 3—Categorize Task

Below are the answers for Practice 1. Check all the items you included in your answer and score yourself.

| Task Activities Summary | Task Category | Give yourself one point for each correct answer |
|---|---|---|
| Smile, make eye contact with guest, acknowledge guest | Sequence | |
| Decide to continue or discontinue current activity | Decision Making | |
| Focus on guest | Sequence | |
| Determine response | Decision Making | |
| | **TOTAL SCORE** | |

If you scored 4, you have correctly completed the task analysis. You may skip Practice 2 and go directly to the **Practice Job Aid Worksheet**. After completing Phase 3—Categorize Task, return to the book for the next phase, Select Format.

If you scored less than 4, you are making progress. Continue to Practice 2 on the next page.

**Go to the next page for Practice 2 for Phase 3—Categorize Task.**

# Practice 2 for Phase 3—Categorize Task

*Target Workers:* Inexperienced claim handlers

*Proper Task Performance:* When taking a recorded statement, the claim handler is expected to:

- State his or her name, the date, the time, and the accident date
- Ask the interviewee to state and spell his or her name and to give permission to take the recorded statement
- Determine the correct questions to ask and how to respond to the replies
- State his or her name and the current time
- Thank the interviewee for giving permission to record the statement

| Task Activities Summary | Task Category |
|---|---|
|  |  |
|  |  |
|  |  |
|  |  |
|  |  |

**When you're ready, go to the next page for the answer key.**

## Answer Key for Practice 2 for Phase 3—Categorize Task

Below are the answers for Practice 2. Check all the items you included in your answer and score yourself.

| Task Activities Summary | Task Category | Give yourself one point for each correct answer |
|---|---|---|
| State name, date, time, loss date; ask interviewee to state and spell name; and give permission to record | Sequence | |
| Ask questions based on interviewee's responses | Decision Making | |
| State name, current time; thank interviewee | Sequence | |
| TOTAL SCORE | | |

If you scored 3, great job. You are ready to work on your **Practice Job Aid Worksheet**. Using your knowledge about how to correctly perform your selected task, complete the Phase 3—Categorize Task. When you are done, return to the book to learn how to select the format.

If you scored less than 3, you might want to review Table 3: Categorize Task before proceeding to your **Practice Job Aid.**

## Practice Job Aid

Go to your **Practice Job Aid Worksheet** on page 68 and categorize your job task.

When completed, return to the book to learn how to select the format for a job aid.

**Go to the next page for Phase 4—Select Format.**

# Phase 4—Select Format

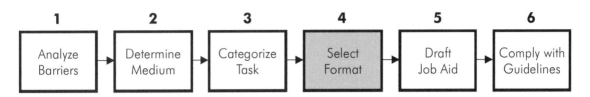

In this phase, you determine which of the following formats or combinations of formats is the correct format for your job aid:

- List
- Fill-in
- Decision Table
- Decision Flowchart

Referring to Table 4: Selecting Format(s) on the next page and Figure 4: Format Examples on the following page, study the case example that follows.

**Go to the next page for Table 4: Selecting Format(s).**

## Table 4: Selecting Format(s)

| IF task category is: | AND | AND | THEN Use Format |
|---|---|---|---|
| Sequence | No written response needed | | List |
| | No written response needed | With three or fewer decisions | Decision Table within a List |
| | No written response needed | With four or more decisions | Decision Flowchart within a List |
| | Written response needed for one or more items in sequence | | List with Fill-in |
| | Written response needed for one or more items in sequence | With three or fewer decisions | Decision Table within a List with Fill-in |
| | Written response needed for one or more items in sequence | With four or more decisions | Decision Flowchart within a List with Fill-in |
| Decision Making | Three or fewer decisions | No written response needed | Decision Table |
| | | Written response needed | Decision Table with Fill-in |
| | | With sequenced steps | List within Decision Table |
| | Four or more decisions | No written response | Decision Flowchart |
| | | Written response needed | Decision Flowchart with Fill-in |
| | | With sequenced steps | List within Decision Flowchart |

**Go to the next page for Figure 4: Format Examples.**

## Figure 4: Format Examples

### List

*Stating full name*

1. State 1st name

2. State 2nd name

3. State last name

---

### List with Fill-in

*Calculating area*

1. Length = _____ feet

2. Width = _____ feet

3. 1 × 2 = _____ square
foot area

---

### Decision Table

*Complying with traffic lights*

| If light is | Then |
|---|---|
| Red | Stop |
| Yellow | Slow Down |
| Green | Go |

---

### List within Decision Table

*Treating a muscle strain*

| If strain occurred | Then |
|---|---|
| ≤6 hours ago | 1. Apply cold 15 minutes <br> 2. Rest 15 minutes <br> 3. Repeat 1 & 2 above |
| >6 hours ago | 1. Apply heat 15 minutes <br> 2. Rest 15 minutes <br> 3. Repeat 1 & 2 above |

---

### Decision Table within List

*How to cook a chicken*

1. Preheat oven to 325°.

2. Remove giblet package.

3. Wash and dry chicken.

4. Put chicken in the oven.

5. 

| If chicken weighs | Then bake |
|---|---|
| ≤6 lbs. | 2 hours |
| >6 lbs. | 2½ hours |

6. Remove from oven.

---

### Decision Table with Fill-in

*Determining affordable housing*

| Neighborhood | Maximum Monthly Payments |
|---|---|
| Executive | Net Income <br><br> $ _____ <br><br> ×    25% <br> ‾‾‾‾‾‾‾‾‾‾ <br> $ _____ <br> Max. Payments |
| Blue Collar | Net Income <br><br> $ _____ <br><br> ×    40% <br> ‾‾‾‾‾‾‾‾‾‾ <br> $ _____ <br> Max. Payments |

---

**Go to next page for more examples.**

## Figure 4: Format Examples *(concluded)*

### Decision Flowchart

*Determining whether training is needed for job aid*

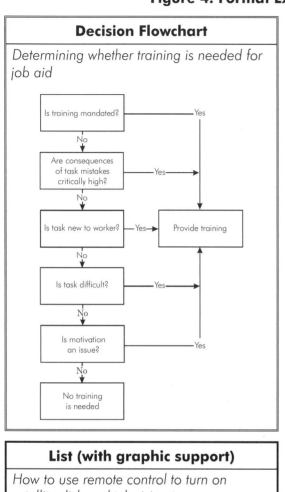

### List within Decision Flowchart

*Ordering items online*

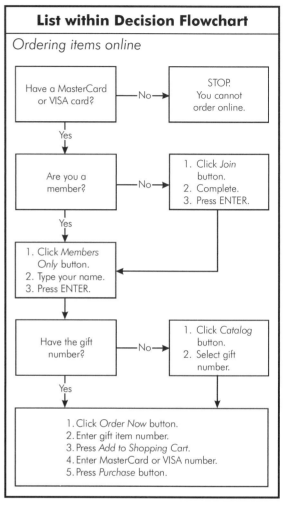

### List (with graphic support)

*How to use remote control to turn on satellite dish and television to use on-screen program menu.*

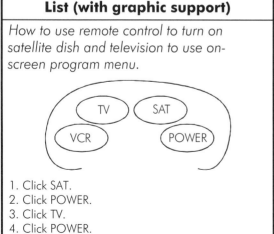

1. Click SAT.
2. Click POWER.
3. Click TV.
4. Click POWER.

**When done, turn the page for a Case Example of Phase 4—Select Format.**

## Case Example for Phase 4—Select Format

Referring to Table 4: Selecting Format(s) and Figure 4: Format Examples, study the case example below.

*Target Workers:* All supervisors

*Task:* Activate the start date for a new hire

*Task Activities:* The supervisor determines a start date that meets both the new hire's needs and the company's needs. Notify the new hire of the start date. Complete Human Resources Form 132 and fax it to Corporate Human Resources.

*Categorize Task:* The first portion of this task involves making fewer than three decisions. The last portion involves correctly completing a sequence.

*Determine Format:* This task involves Decision Making then a Sequence. Written responses are not required. The job aid should be Decision Table followed by a List.

**Go to the next page for Practice 1 for Phase 4—Select Format.**

## Practice 1 for Phase 4—Select Format

Referring to Table 4: Select Format(s) and Figure 4: Format Examples, complete Column C and Column D based on the information provided.

*Target Workers:* Receptionists

*Task:* Receptionist's appropriate performance when a guest enters the reception area

| COLUMN A | COLUMN B | COLUMN C | COLUMN D |
|---|---|---|---|
| Task Activities Summary | Sequence/ Decision Making | Number of Steps or Decisions | Format |
| Smile, make eye contact with guest, acknowledge guest | Sequence | | |
| Decide to continue or discontinue current activity | Decision Making | | |
| Focus on guest | Sequence | | |
| Through a series of questions and knowledge of company, determine satisfactory response | Decision Making | | |

**When you're ready, go to the next page for the answer key.**

# Answer Key for Practice 1 for Phase 4—Select Format

Below are the correct answers to Practice 1. Compare these with your answers

| COLUMN A | COLUMN B | COLUMN C | COLUMN D |
|---|---|---|---|
| **Task Activities Summary** | **Sequence/ Decision Making** | **Number of Steps or Decisions** | **Format** |
| Smile, make eye contact with guest, acknowledge guest | Sequence | 3 | List |
| Decide to continue or discontinue current job | Decision Making | 1 | **Decision Table** |
| Focus on guest | Sequence | 1 | List |
| Through a series of questions and knowledge of company, determine satisfactory response | Decision Making | **4 or more** | **Decision Flowchart** |

How did you do? If your answer was completely correct, great job! Go to Practice 2 to find out how you might handle a different task.

If your answer was not completely correct, review the previous material before continuing to Practice 2. You're doing fine.

**Go to the next page for Practice 2 for Phase 4—Select Format.**

## Practice 2 for Phase 4—Select Format

Referring to Table 4: Select Format(s) and Figure 4: Format Examples, complete Column C and Column D based on the information provided.

*Target Workers:* Claim trainees

*Task:* Claim handler taking a recorded statement

| COLUMN A | COLUMN B | COLUMN C | COLUMN D |
| --- | --- | --- | --- |
| Task Activities Summary | Sequence/ Decision Making | Number of Steps or Decisions | Format |
| State own name, current date and time, and loss date. Ask interviewee to state and spell name and to give permission to record. | Sequence | | |
| Determine series of questions based on interviewee's responses. | Decision Making | | |
| State own name and current time, confirm it was recorded, and thank the interviewee. | Sequence | | |

**When you're ready, go to the next page for the answer key.**

# Answer Key for Practice 2 for Phase 4—Select Format

Below are the correct answers to Practice 2. Compare these with your answers.

*Target Workers:* Claim trainees

*Task:* Claim handler taking a recorded statement

| COLUMN A | COLUMN B | COLUMN C | COLUMN D |
|---|---|---|---|
| Task Activities Summary | Sequence/ Decision Making | Number of Steps or Decisions | Format |
| State own name, current date and time, and loss date. Ask interviewee to state and spell name and to give permission to record. | Sequence | 6 | List |
| Determine series of questions based on interviewee's responses. | Decision Making | 4 or more | Decision Flowchart |
| State own name and current time, confirm it was recorded, and thank the interviewee. | Sequence | 4 | List |

Did your answers match the answer key?

If they did, you have done an excellent job on this complex task. You may skip Practice 3 and go directly to the **Practice Job Aid**. When you complete selecting the format, return to the book to learn about Phase 5—Draft Job Aid.

If your answers differ significantly from the answer key, don't be discouraged. This is a complex task. Try the practice problem on the next page.

**Go to the next page for Practice 3 for Phase 4—Select Format.**

## Practice 3 for Phase 4—Select Format

Referring to Table 4: Select Format(s) and Figure 4: Format Examples, complete Column C and Column D based on the information provided.

*Target Workers:* All trainers

*Task:* Arrange for a training event to be delivered by a vendor.

- Ask vendor for preferred dates for presentation, maximum number of participants, location of training, and size of classroom.
- Select the date for the training along with the most cost-effective way to meet the vendor's needs.
- Complete Form #321—Summary of Training Arrangements.
- Send the completed form to the vendor.

| COLUMN A | COLUMN B | COLUMN C | COLUMN D |
|---|---|---|---|
| **Task Activities Summary** | **Sequence/ Decision Making** | **Number of Steps or Decisions** | **Format** |
| Ask vendor for preferred dates for presentation, maximum number of participants, location of training, and size of classroom. | Sequence | | |
| Determine how to best meet vendor's request for preferred dates for presentation, maximum number of participants, location of training, and size of classroom. | Decision Making | | |
| Complete Form #321— Summary of Training Arrangements. Send the completed form to the vendor. | Sequence | | |

**When you're ready, go to the next page for the answer key.**

# Answer Key for Practice 3 for Phase 4—Select Format

Below are the correct answers to Practice 3. Compare these with your answers.

| COLUMN A<br>Task Activities Summary | COLUMN B<br>Sequence/ Decision Making | COLUMN C<br>Number of Steps or Decisions | COLUMN D<br>Format |
|---|---|---|---|
| Ask vendor for preferred dates for presentation, maximum number of participants, location of training, and size of classroom. | Sequence | 3 | List |
| Determine how to best meet vendor's request for preferred dates for presentation, maximum number of participants, location of training, and size of classroom. | Decision Making | 4 or more | Decision Flowchart |
| Complete Form #321— Summary of Training Arrangements.<br><br>Send the completed form to the vendor. | Sequence | 2 | List |

If your answers are correct, congratulations! You are ready to work on your **Practice Job Aid**. After you select your aid format, return to the book to learn how to draft your job aid.

If your answer was not correct, you might want to review the course material before continuing with your **Practice Job Aid**.

**This was the last practice for this phase.**

## Practice Job Aid

Go to your **Practice Job Aid Worksheet** on page 69 and select the format for your job aid.

After you complete this step, return to the book to learn how to draft a job aid.

**Go to the next page for Phase 5—Draft Job Aid.**

# Phase 5—Draft Job Aid

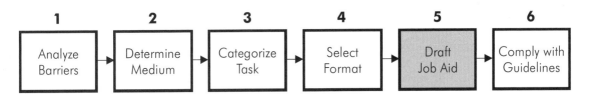

| 1 | 2 | 3 | 4 | 5 | 6 |
|---|---|---|---|---|---|
| Analyze Barriers | Determine Medium | Categorize Task | Select Format | Draft Job Aid | Comply with Guidelines |

Complete all the previous phases before drafting your job aid.

Below is an example of a properly drafted stand-alone, hard-copy job aid in the fill-in format.

## Case Example for Phase 5—Draft Job Aid

| | Task Activities to Determine Instructor Costs to Deliver a Classroom Training Session | |
|---|---|---|
| **Step** | **Information Requested** | **Write Response** |
| 1 | Instructor's salary plus benefits/hour | |
| 2 | Total hours to prepare for training, travel to training site, and deliver training | |
| 3 | Multiply Steps 1 and 2 | |
| 4 | Travel and hotel costs | |
| 5 | Add Steps 3 and 4 | |
| 6 | Material and facility costs | |
| 7 | Add Steps 5 and 6 | \$_____ <br> TOTAL COST |

**Go to the next page for Practice 1 for Phase 5—Draft Job Aid.**

## Practice 1 for Phase 5—Draft Job Aid

Referring to the previous material, complete the analyses below and draft a job aid for the following job.

*Target Workers:* Human Resource trainers

*Task:* Grading students after the training module, "Customer Service for the Receptionist"

*Task Activity Summary:* To receive an A, the student must score 90% or higher on the written test and get a satisfactory rating on the role-play exercise. To get a B, the student must score 80%–89% on the written test and get a satisfactory rating on the role-play exercise. To get a C, the student must score 70%–79% on the written test and get a satisfactory rating on the role-play. The student fails if the written test score is less than 70% or the student gets an unsatisfactory rating on the role-play exercise.

*Phase 1.*  *Analyze Barriers*

Physical Barriers? _____

People Barriers? _____

Create a job aid? _____

*Phase 2.*  *Select Medium*

Computer-Based or Hard-Copy? _____

Integrated or Stand-Alone? _____

*Phase 3.*  *Categorize Task* and *Phase 4. Select Format*

| Task Activities Summary | Task Category | Number of Steps or Decisions | Format |
|---|---|---|---|
|  |  |  |  |
|  |  |  |  |

**Continued on the next page.**

*Phase 5.  Draft Job Aid*

If you turned the page before drafting the job aid, please go back and complete Practice 1 for Phase 5—Draft Job Aid.

You might find this frustrating; many people do at the beginning.

Don't give up. This practice is very important.

It really is not as easy as it looks at first, so take your time.

**When you're ready, go to the next the page for the answer key.**

## Answer Key for Practice 1 for Phase 5—Draft Job Aid

Below are the correct answers to Practice 1. Compare these with your answers.

*Phase 1.* *Analyze Barriers*

Physical Barriers? **None since the instructor can select setting.**

People Barriers? **None because the instructor will be alone.**

Create a job aid? **Yes.**

*Phase 2.* *Select Media*

Computer-Based or Hard-Copy? **Hard-copy because job is not computer-related.**

Integrated or Stand-Alone? **Integrated into Instructor's Guide so the job aid cannot be easily misplaced.**

*Phase 3.* *Categorize Task* and *Phase 4. Select Format*

| Task Activities Summary | Task Category | Number of Steps or Decisions | Format |
|---|---|---|---|
| Determine whether student got a satisfactory role-play rating. Then, determine test grade. | Decision Making | 2 | Decision Table |

*Phase 5.* *Draft Job Aid*

| IF student: | AND scored: | THEN grade is: |
|---|---|---|
| Got a **satisfactory** rating on the role-play exercise | 90% or higher on test | A |
| | 80%–89% on test | B |
| | 70%–79% on test | C |
| Got an **unsatisfactory** rating on the role-play exercise | ---------------------- | Failing |

How did it go?

If you had the correct answers, you're doing great. Turn the page for Practice 2 for Phase 5—Draft Job Aid.

If your answers did not match the answer key, don't be discouraged. This was your first try at applying all the phases up to and including Draft Job Aid. This is not an easy process. Before going to Practice 2 for Phase 5—Draft Job Aid, you might want to review the previous material.

**Go to the next page for Practice 2 for Phase 5—Draft Job Aid.**

## Practice 2 for Phase 5—Draft Job Aid

Referring to the previous material, complete the analyses below and draft a job aid for the following job.

*Target Workers:* Human Resources trainers

*Task:* Preparing the classroom for "Customer Service for the Receptionist"

*Task Activities:* Be sure the tables are set up in a U-shape. Set out a table tent and name tag at each seat. Make sure the overhead projector works. Place a flipchart with three color markers at the front of the class.

*Phase 1.*   *Analyze Barriers*

        Physical Barriers? _____

        People Barriers? _____

        Create a job aid? _____

*Phase 2.*   *Select Media*

        Computer-Based or Hard-Copy? _____

        Integrated or Stand-Alone? _____

*Phase 3.*   *Categorize Task* and *Phase 4. Select Format*

| Task Activities Summary | Task Category | Number of Steps or Decisions | Format |
|---|---|---|---|
|  |  |  |  |
|  |  |  |  |

*Phase 5.*   *Draft Job Aid*

|  |
|---|
|  |

**When you're ready, go to the next page for the answer key.**

# Answer Key for Practice 2 for Phase 5—Draft Job Aid

Below are the correct answers to Practice 2. Compare these with your answers.

*Phase 1.* *Analyze Barriers*

    Physical Barriers?     None.

    People Barriers?     None since worker will be alone.

    Create a job aid?     **Yes.**

*Phase 2.* *Select Media*

    Computer-Based or Hard-Copy?     **Hard-copy because job is not computer-related.**

    Integrated or Stand-Alone?     **Integrated into Facilitator's Guide so the job aid cannot be easily misplaced.**

*Phase 3.* *Categorize Task* and *Phase 4. Select Format*

| Task Activities Summary | Task Category | Number of Steps or Decisions | Format |
|---|---|---|---|
| Be sure the tables are set up in a U-shape.<br><br>Set out a table tent and name tag at each seat.<br><br>Make sure the overhead projector works.<br><br>Place a flipchart with three color markers at the front of the class. | Sequence | 4 | List |

*Phase 5.* *Draft Job Aid*

> **How to prepare classroom for "Customer Service for Receptionists."**
> 1. Be sure the tables are set up in a U-shape.
> 2. Set out a table tent and name tag at each seat.
> 3. Make sure the overhead projector works.
> 4. Place a flipchart with three color markers at the front of the class.

How did your answers compare with the answer key?

If you selected the List format, congratulations. You have correctly completed the most important aspect of this practice.

**Go to the next page.**

## Practice Job Aid

Now it is time to actually draft your **Practice Job Aid**.

Referring to the course material covered so far, go to your **Practice Job Aid Worksheet** on page 70 and draft your job aid.

**Go to the next page for Phase 6—Comply with Guidelines.**

# Phase 6—Comply with Guidelines

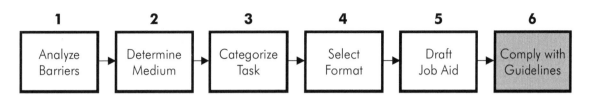

To do this, first edit the job aid to comply with the Format Guidelines (see Table 6.1 below). Next, edit the job aid to comply with the General Guidelines (see Table 6.2 on page 54).

## Table 6.1: Format Guidelines

| Format | Guidelines |
|--------|-----------|
| List | • Use for sequential behavior.<br>• Number or letter the steps in order.<br>• If there is no preferred order for the steps, assign an order.<br>• Use drawings only when worker interacts with an object; conducts a physical act; has poor reading skills.<br>• Set off steps with boxes, horizontal lines, or white space.<br>• Put all information for one step on the same page.<br>• If you are not sure that the explanation is thorough, add more detail.<br>• Use words the worker knows. |
| Fill-in | • Use when a written response on the job aid is required.<br>• Put response area after the desired activity.<br>• Provide sufficient room for the worker's response.<br>• Put items in the order they are completed to reduce worker's eye movements when using job aid.<br>• Keep reusable worksheets separate. |

**Continued on next page.**

**Table 6.1: Format Guidelines** *(concluded)*

| Format | Guidelines |
|---|---|
| Decision-Table | • Use when task involves no more than three decisions.<br>• Use a table format.<br>• Sequence in preferred order of decision making.<br>• List the IF's and AND's before the THEN's.<br>• Simplify the table as much as possible. |
| Decision-Flowchart | • Use when task involves more than three decisions.<br>• Use action verbs.<br>• Provide a yes response box and a no response box for each question box.<br>• Strive to keep the flowchart on one page.<br>• Simplify the flowchart as much as possible.<br>• Minimize worker's eye movements.<br>• Keep decision lines from crossing over each other.<br>• Put the most frequently selected or most important decision first. |

**Go to the next page for a Case Example of Phase 6—Comply with Guidelines.**

Referring to Table 6.1: Format Guidelines on the previous pages, study the case example below.

## Case Example for Phase 6—Comply with Format Guidelines

We are now using a new computer software help desk provider.
You will experience improved service by following the directions below.

Understand the problem.
Know your employer code and user ID.
Call the help desk @ 1-888-888-1515.
If asked to wait, do not hang up.
Affirm your employee code and user ID.
Clearly describe the problem.
Follow the help desk's instructions.

There are three list format errors in the above case example.

1. Steps are not numbered.

2. Photograph adds no value and should be deleted.

3. More white space is needed between the steps.

**Go to the next page for Practice 1 for
Phase 6—Comply with Format Guidelines.**

## Practice 1 for Phase 6—Comply with Format Guidelines

Referring to Table 6.1: Format Guidelines, list three errors in this Decision-Flowchart.

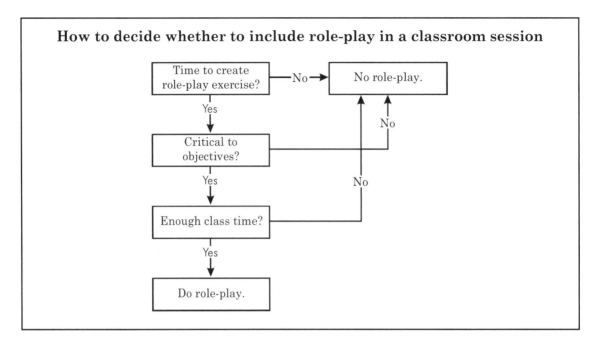

List three errors in the above Decision-Flowchart.

1. _____

2. _____

3. _____

**When you're ready, go to the next page for the answer key.**

## Answer Key for Practice 1 for
## Phase 6—Comply with Format Guidelines

Below are the answers for Practice 1. Compare these to your answers.

List three errors in the Decision-Flowchart.

1. **Action verbs are not used.**
2. **Worker's eye movements are excessive.**
3. **The decision lines cross over each other.**

How did you do?

If your answers match the answer key, good work. Now try your hand with a different format in Practice 2.

If your answers do not match the answer key, be sure to carefully study Table 6.1: Format Guidelines when developing a Decision-Flowchart job aid.

**Go to the next page for Practice 2 for
Phase 6—Comply with Format Guidelines.**

## Practice 2 for Phase 6—Comply with Format Guidelines

Referring to Table 6.1: Format Guidelines, identify three errors in the Fill-in format below to comply with Format Guidelines.

| Determine Instructor Costs to Deliver a Classroom Training Session | | |
|---|---|---|
| **Step** | **Response** | **Information Requested** |
| 1 | | Instructor's salary plus benefits/hour |
| 2 | | Total hours to prepare for training, travel to training site, and deliver training |
| 3 | | Travel and hotel costs |
| 4 | | Material and facility costs |
| 5 | | Multiply Steps 1 and 2 |
| 6 | | Add Steps 3 and 4 |

List three errors in the above Fill-in format.

1. _____

2. _____

3. _____

**When you're ready, go to the next page for the answer key.**

## Answer Key for Practice 2 for
## Phase 6—Comply with Format Guidelines

List three errors in the Fill-in format.

1. **Response area is before, instead of after, the activity.**
2. **The steps are not in the proper sequence.**
3. **The response areas are too small.**

If you had the same responses as the answer key, congratulations!

If not, be sure to refer to Table 6.1: Format Guidelines when creating a Fill-in Job Aid.

**Go to the next page for Practice 3 for
Phase 6—Comply with Format Guidelines.**

## Practice 3 for Phase 6—Comply with Format Guidelines

Referring to Table 6.1: Format Guidelines, identify two errors in this Decision-Table.

| Determine Bonus Percentage | | |
|---|---|---|
| **Bonus Percentage** | **IF performance is** | **AND employee is** |
| 5% | Superior | Manager |
| 3% | Satisfactory | Manager |
| 4% | Superior | Technician |
| 2% | Satisfactory | Technician |
| 0% | Unsatisfactory | Manager |
| 0% | Unsatisfactory | Technician |

List two errors in the above Decision-Table.

1. _____

2. _____

**When you're ready, go to the next page for the answer key.**

## Answer Key for Practice 3 for
## Phase 6—Comply with Format Guidelines

Below are the answers for Practice 3. Compare these with your answers.

List two errors in the above Decision-Table.

1. **The columns are not in the correct order. They should be IF-AND-THEN, not THEN-IF-AND.**
2. **The list of options is not in a logical order.**

If you didn't get both answers, take a moment to review Table 6.1: Format Guidelines for the Decision-Table Format.

**The other part of Phase 6 is to Comply with General Guidelines.**

To do this, edit the Job Aid to comply with the General Guidelines shown in Table 6.2 on the next page.

**Go to the next page for Table 6.2: General Guidelines.**

## Table 6.2: General Guidelines

| General Guidelines that Apply to All Formats: List, Fill-in, Decision-Table, and Decision-Flowchart |
|---|
| • Place job title first. |
| • Verify content is correct. |
| • Avoid vague terms such as understand, often, etc. |
| • Use simple words in short sentences. |
| • Use action verbs instead of phrases or passive verbs. |
| • Avoid extensive background information. |
| • Use of color text or graphics only if the job involves color discrimination. |
| • Put condition before action. |
| • Avoid photographs and complex drawings. |
| • Scale drawings to fit the page. |
| • Put drawings to the left or above the related information. |
| • Be generous with white space. |
| • Draw notice to negative words such as **never** and **not** by putting word in bold and/or all capital letters. |
| • Draw notice to conditional words such as **WHEN** and **IF** by putting word in bold and/or all capital letters. |
| • Put important points in boxes to highlight. |
| • Use symbols such as arrows to direct target worker. |
| • Combine formats as needed to explain the task. |
| • Avoid humor. It is distracting. |

**Go to the next page for a Case Example for Phase 6—Comply with General Guidelines.**

## Case Example for Phase 6—Comply with General Guidelines

> Request help for computer software problems.
>
> 1. Understand the problem.
> 2. Know your employer code and user ID.
> 3. Call the help desk @ 1-888-888-1515.
> 4. If asked to wait, do not hang up.
> 5. Affirm your employee code and user ID.
> 6. Clearly describe the problem.
> 7. Follow the help desk's instructions.

The following changes are needed to the case example for Phase 6—Comply with General Guidelines:

1. Replace vague words with clear words; for example, change "Understand" to "Identify" in Step 1 and "know" to "locate" in Step 2.

2. Use simple words; for example, replace "affirm" with "state" in Step 5.

3. Box Step 3 since it is essential to dial the correct number.

4. Capitalize and/or bold the word "not" in Step 4.

There is only one practice for Phase 6—Comply with General Guidelines.

**Continued on the next page.**

## Practice 1 for Phase 6—Comply with General Guidelines

Referring to Table 6.2: General Guidelines and the case example, identify two changes that should be made to the Fill-in job aid below.

| Step | Information | Write Response |
|------|-------------|----------------|
| \multicolumn{3}{c}{**Determine the Cost of Instructor-led Training**} | | |
| 1 | Instructor's salary plus benefits/hour | |
| 2 | Total hours to prepare for training, travel to training site, and deliver training | |
| 3 | Multiply Steps 1 and 2 | |
| 4 | Travel and hotel costs | |
| 5 | Add Steps 3 and 4 | |
| 6 | Material and facility costs | |
| 7 | Add Steps 5 and 6 | \$_____ <br> TOTAL COST |

List two changes that should be made to the above Fill-in job aid.

1. _____

2. _____

**When you're ready, go to the next page for the answer key.**

## Answer Key for Practice 1 for
## Phase 6—Comply with General Guidelines

Below are the answers for Practice 1. Compare these with your answers.

Two changes that should be made to the Fill-in job aid.

1. **Begin phrases with action verbs; for example, "Calculate travel and hotel costs," instead of "Travel and hotel costs" in Step 4.**
2. **Add white space to each column or increase font size.**

Did you get both answers?

If not, be sure to refer to Table 6.2: General Guidelines when editing a job aid.

## Practice Job Aid

Now it's time to complete your job aid. Go to your **Practice Job Aid Worksheet** on page 71, refer to Table 6.1: Format Guidelines and Table 6.2: General Guidelines, and edit your job aid draft.

After that, create your final job aid.

**Go to the next page for general suggestions on successfully implementing a job aid.**

# Suggestions for Creating and Implementing Job Aids

When implementing job aids, involve management at the start. Demonstrate how the job aid can improve performance and reduce costs.

Before announcing and distributing any job aid, be sure to do the following:

1. Create a clean version using graphics experts or software such as Visio Professional or Inspiration.
2. Have peers review the completed job aid for clarity and correctness.
3. Pilot the job aid with a random sampling of the target workers.
4. Revise the job aid as needed based on the pilot target workers' feedback.
5. Determine whether the target workers need to be trained and/or motivated in using the job aid. If the decision to either is yes, prepare training and/or motivational activity.

When presenting any job aid to management or target workers, avoid adult education terms such as "job aid" and "task aid." Instead, call it a cheat sheet, training aid, reference sheet, etc.

**Good luck creating future job aids!**

# The Next Step

Where do **you** go from here? Take time to consider the ideas below:

❏ Evaluate an existing job aid and improve it. This is an excellent way to practice your skills without taking on the entire design process.

❏ Select a current personal or business task of yours that would be easier to complete with a job aid. Try your hand at it. Be sure to start with a simpler task as you build your skill.

❏ Offer to create a simple job aid to help a visually impaired person complete a common task such as reheating a meal in a microwave oven or playing a particular CD-ROM. This will challenge your creativity. It will also ease the life of another!

❏ Keep a log of job aids you see in one week. They are everywhere. Check out fast-food restaurants for instance. This will broaden your arsenal of possible formats for job aids.

❏ Identify someone in management who you think would be open to the creation and use of job aids. Offer your services to create one for this person. Building champions and sponsors is important.

❏ If you are a trainer, select one of your popular sessions and create a job aid the students can take away with them. This is an excellent way to promote the transition of learning to the workplace.

❏ If you are a manager, identify a performance gap in one of your direct reports that concerns you. Consider a job aid as a possible part of the intervention.

❏ If you write reference manuals, select a task that is frequently done incorrectly and change that portion of the manual to a job aid.

❏ Create a job aid for a child to complete a new task such as making a bed. This will challenge your ability to clearly explain a task and effectively separate motivation from the role of the job aid.

❏ Teach someone how to create a simple job aid. By teaching another, you reinforce for yourself how to do the process properly.

❏ Brainstorm different ways to use job aids; for example, how to guide a decision process in general.

❏ List ten different names for job aids. Often the choice of the label you select can affect the customer's acceptance of the job aid.

# Appendix A: Practice Job Aid Worksheet

# Practice Job Aid Worksheet

*Permission is granted to copy the Practice Job Aid Worksheet for personal use only.*

Write a simple task below:

_____

_____

_____

_____

State and describe your Target Workers:

_____

_____

_____

_____

**Return to Page 1 of the Book**

**When directed, complete Phase 1—Analyze Barriers for your Practice Job Aid.**

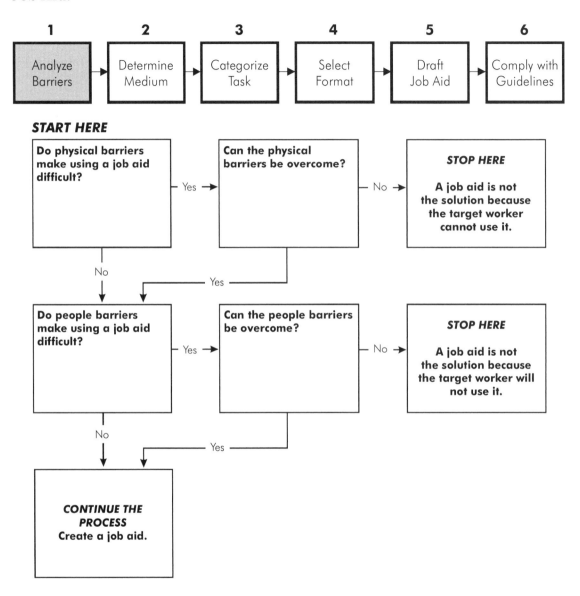

If your decision is not to create a job aid, select another task.

---

**Return to Book**

---

**When directed, complete Phase 2—Determine Medium for your Practice Job Aid.**

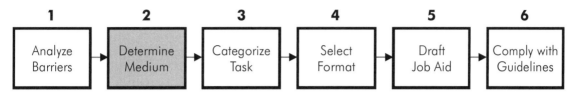

| Medium | Your Decision |
|---|---|
| Computer-based? | |
| Hard-copy? | |
| Integrated? | |
| Stand-alone? | |
| **Your Media Decision** | |

**Return to Book**

**When directed, complete Phase 3—Categorize Task for your Practice Job Aid.**

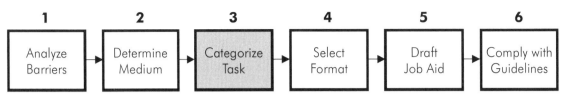

| Task Activities Summary | Task Category |
|---|---|
| | |
| | |
| | |
| | |
| | |
| | |
| | |
| | |
| | |
| | |

**Return to Book**

## When directed, complete Phase 4—Select Format for your Practice Job Aid.

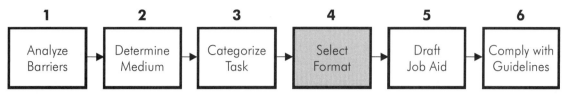

| 1 | 2 | 3 | 4 | 5 | 6 |
|---|---|---|---|---|---|
| Analyze Barriers | Determine Medium | Categorize Task | Select Format | Draft Job Aid | Comply with Guidelines |

| Task Categories from Phase 3 | Number of Steps or Decisions | Format |
|---|---|---|
|  |  |  |
|  |  |  |
|  |  |  |
|  |  |  |
|  |  |  |
|  |  |  |
|  |  |  |

**Return to Book**

**When directed, complete Phase 5—Draft Job Aid for your Practice Job Aid.**

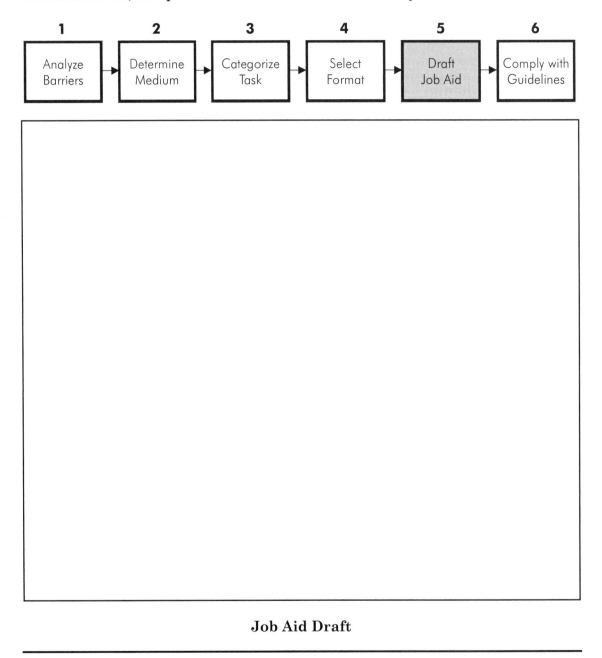

**Job Aid Draft**

**Return to Book**

**When directed, complete Phase 6—Comply with Guidelines for your Practice Job Aid.**

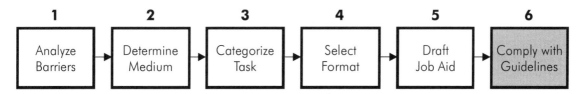

Return to your draft on the previous page and edit to comply with both Format Guidelines and General Guidelines.

## CONGRATULATIONS!

## Return to Book

# Appendix B:
# A Case Example

# Purpose of this Case Example

This case example will help you apply the process covered in this book by illustrating the entire process in context—from initial request to objective results.

## The Initial Request

Jack, the rental manager in a large real estate management company, contacted Mary, a corporate trainer. He wanted her to design and deliver a half-day training program on how to post the receipt of delinquent payments on their rental properties countrywide.

Jack explained that his most knowledgeable worker, Jan, was frequently taken from her supervisory duties to answer delinquent payment entry questions. In addition, the computer records were full of errors and it was taking too much of his staff's time to correct them. In some cases, the payment records were so incomplete that the delinquent payments were not even credited to the company's bottom line. The financial loss was estimated to be in the tens of thousands.

## The Target Audience

Mary's first step was to accurately identify the target audience. Jack explained that their regional clerks entered the delinquent rent payments. Most of these clerks have at least five years experience as entry clerks and know the company's computer systems well. Most are high school graduates. On average, a regional clerk processes two delinquent rent payments per week.

## The Design Team

Mary made no commitment to create training. Instead, she told Jack that to customize the intervention, she would need to learn more about the entry process. She asked Jack if Jan, the experienced worker who fields most of the calls, could partner with her.

The purpose of this request was threefold. First, Mary could be assured that the technical content would be accurate. Second, Jan would have a great deal to gain from improved performance at the regional level (this is important since the analysis phase can take considerable time and patience). Finally, as a valued employee, the experienced worker could serve as Mary's supporting link to Jack. Jan, the central payments supervisor, was more than happy to help.

Next, Mary worked with Jan and Jack to identify all parties who had an active interest in the delinquent payment process. Mary knew how important it is to get all appropriate parties involved as soon as possible. This helps assure the completeness and accuracy of the data as well as avoid unpleasant surprises later. An identified key player in the delinquent payment process was David, the security manager. His job, to protect the company's assets, generated a keen interest in the security of checks and cash. David was happy to act as an advisor on the project.

Finally, Mary asked Jan to identify two or three regional clerks of average ability who would be willing to help with the project. They were notified and added to the design team. These clerks would be very useful in getting information about the work process and environment as well as piloting the intervention.

## Data on the Task

David, the security manager, Jan, and Mary identified all existing documentation on the entry of delinquent payments into the company's computer system. Three documents were found. One dealt with the importance of proper entry. The second dealt with security issues. The third described the responsibilities of each person in the process. These were certainly useful documents, but none explained exactly *how* to process the entry.

Mary asked Jan to show her how to properly process a payment. Jan was eager to help and said the entry system was easy. By taking notes and asking questions, Mary revealed a complex process with multiple unguided decision points. The system was far from intuitive. Because of her high competence with the system, the expert had made incorrect assumptions about the ease of the task and had communicated her frustration on the work quality to Jack.

## The Performance Gap

Mary asked Jan to identify the skills, knowledge, and attitudes needed to properly complete the delinquent check payment entry process. Jan felt that all the regional clerks had the computer skills to complete the process, but lacked the knowledge of exactly how to complete the entry. Jan also felt that the regional clerks wanted to do the work accurately since their bonuses were tied to the accuracy of their entries. Mary spoke with the regional clerks on the design team and found that Jan's assessment was correct.

Mary and Jan agreed that the true performance gap was exclusively in the knowledge on how to complete the process.

## Transitioning Customer to Job Aid Solution

During this process, Mary and Jan kept Jack "in the loop" and shared with him the complexity of the entry process. They also stated that the regional clerks had the skills to complete the process if they were given proper guidance and information. Jack began to voice the idea that perhaps this was not really a training issue. Mary was pleased that he recognized this. They agreed to complete the process documentation and then re-evaluate the training need.

## Phase 1. Analyze Barriers

Mary visited a typical regional office to identify any issues that might bar or inhibit a regional clerk from using instructions when completing the delinquent payment entry process. She found their workstations were well lit with sufficient space to place job aids. The regional clerks stated that they constantly had to learn and apply new procedures, so there was no expectation that anyone could complete all tasks without written reminders. She even found cheat sheets the clerks had created themselves; unfortunately, there were none on completing the delinquent payment entry process. When Mary asked the regional clerks about the lack of cheat sheets for delinquent payment entry, the clerks said there did not seem to be any logic to the process. Later, Jan confirmed that all the regional offices were very similar to the one Mary visited.

Since there were no barriers to using aids, Mary and Jan agreed to create a job aid. Jack was advised and supported the initiative.

## Phase 2. Determine Medium

Since the regional clerks were constantly using their computers, Jan suggested making the job aid computer-based, and Mary agreed that this was logical. They were concerned, however, when they found that due to system incompatibilities, the instructions could not be viewed at the same time as the work screen. Since the process was lengthy, they felt it would be frustrating for the regional clerk to keep switching back and forth between systems.

On the other hand, Mary and Jan felt a hard-copy form could easily become mislaid with all the other paper. They also anticipated some improvements to the process that would require the instructions to be updated. Therefore, they decided the best medium for this situation was an online form because it could be easily modified and distributed. In addition, the regional clerks would be instructed to print the form when processing delinquent payments.

Since the process was not part of a larger job, they decided to keep the instructions as a stand-alone.

## Phase 3. Categorize Task

Mary carefully studied the rough draft of the instructions for completing the delinquent payment entry process and found it was a series of decision-making events in a predetermined sequence of steps.

## Phase 4. Select Format

The delinquent payment entry process involves more than four decisions in a specified sequence. Since the regional clerks also had to gather information from other sources, Mary felt it would be helpful to provide space to write the information rather than have the regional clerks memorize it. To meet these needs, Mary selected a combined format of Lists within a Decision Flowchart with Fill-Ins.

## Phase 5. Draft Job Aid

The time had finally come to draft the job aid. While documenting the data, Mary found that simply printing screens and making notes on the printouts were not sufficient. She began to add sticky notes and cross-references to the printed screens, but even this became difficult to follow.

As the full scope of the process revealed itself, Mary had a choice of simplifying the process or using a diagramming software. Mary knew from experience that it is always best to include details when in doubt. Therefore, to capture the details, she used Visio Professional™ for Microsoft Windows.

Mary and Jan spent 20 hours over two weeks reducing the entire process to writing. Decision points, information gaps, and information sources were also identified and added to the process. Both Mary and Jan became frustrated with the amount of time it took. Fortunately, each had a break while the other either edited the draft or corrected the document.

In addition, Mary asked David, the security manager, to edit the job aid and provide any clarifying language around the integrated security steps. He found an inconsistent use of a term, but otherwise approved the job aid.

Finally, under Jan's watchful eye, Mary referred to the job aid draft and tried to complete the entry process using different scenarios. When Mary, who had limited data-entry experience, correctly completed the entry process, they decided to celebrate and share the job aid with Jack.

Jack was impressed that Mary could complete the job just by referring to the three-page instruction sheet. He wanted to publish the instructions immediately. Mary and Jan suggested getting the entire design team's approval before posting the instructions on the company's intranet. Jack agreed and was pleased with the outcome. He no longer asked about training.

## Phase 6. Comply with Guidelines

Mary made sure each step was boxed with sufficient white space to provide a clean, simple look. Words were selected carefully and used consistently.

Fill-in spaces were provided when needed with at least one-third of an inch of vertical space to hand write the information.

She scrutinized the verbs to ensure that they were action verbs. Arrows followed each decision point. Mary also traced with a pencil her eye movements as she followed the process instructions. With this information, she rearranged the job aid to eliminate unnecessary eye movements.

Mary knew that grammatical and spelling errors could discredit the job aid in the eyes of the regional clerks and her customer, Jack. After editing the job aid many times herself, Mary realized that the document had become too familiar to her to identify any additional errors. She then asked another trainer and a regional clerk to proofread the job aid. They found several typographical errors.

## Pilot

The job aid was now ready to be piloted. First Mary observed two regional clerks using the job aid while completing the actual work in a regional office. Mary was available to answer questions, but offered no advice. The work went well except that both clerks felt intimidated by the flowchart. As a result, no actual changes needed to be made to the job aid.

The instructions were then mailed to a random sample of regional clerks. After each regional clerk used the guide, Mary and Jan conducted telephone debriefs. As in the observations, the regional clerks successfully completed the delinquent payment entry process, but several felt the format was more appropriate for college graduates.

## Training and Delivery

During the pilot, the regional clerks expressed a lack of confidence in working with flowcharts. Since the regional clerks were widely dispersed, Mary recommended a self-study module on how to read instructions flowcharts and to help the regional clerks realize that they use flowcharts (perhaps unknowingly) when making decisions every day of their lives. The sole purpose of this training was to increase the regional clerks' confidence in working with flowcharts.

To promote compliance, the rental company's president and the regional office managers jointly announced the new "Delinquent Check Entry Process Instructions." Mary had decided to use the term *instructions* since the regional clerks commonly used this word themselves.

## Objective Results

Three months after launching the job aid and its limited training, the regional clerks reported no frustration with completing the delinquent payment entry process and were looking forward to better appraisals. Jan reported a marked drop in calls for routine help. When a regional clerk did call, the questions were unique.

After six months, the percentage of errors decreased by 90% with a savings of $50,000.

In addition, the hard cost savings of using a job aid instead of training to address the performance gap was estimated to be $40,000. This did not address the retraining that Mary felt would have been needed due to the infrequency with which the regional clerks conducted the process.

## Conclusion

By carefully gathering data, precisely identifying the target audience, and clearly describing the performance gap, Mary determined a job aid was the best solution for this particular problem. By working continuously and cooperatively with the customer who requested training, she also promoted and nurtured management support for this alternative solution.

Her early attention to all interested parties helped Mary ensure that the job aid would be effective and supported. Finally, the well-executed pilot identified a training issue that could have sabotaged the effectiveness of the job aid if it had not been recognized.

Of course, job aids are not the best solution for all requests for training or performance improvement; however, this solution is too frequently not considered. Not thinking about job aids can result in expensive and ineffective training, disgruntled customers, and lost profits.

On the following three pages is the job aid that was created in this case study.

# Delinquent Payment Entry Instructions

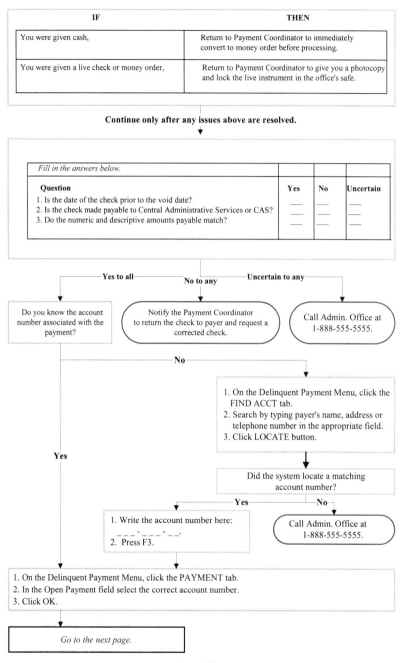

| IF | THEN |
|---|---|
| You were given cash, | Return to Payment Coordinator to immediately convert to money order before processing. |
| You were given a live check or money order, | Return to Payment Coordinator to give you a photocopy and lock the live instrument in the office's safe. |

**Continue only after any issues above are resolved.**

*Fill in the answers below.*

| Question | Yes | No | Uncertain |
|---|---|---|---|
| 1. Is the date of the check prior to the void date? | ___ | ___ | ___ |
| 2. Is the check made payable to Central Administrative Services or CAS? | ___ | ___ | ___ |
| 3. Do the numeric and descriptive amounts payable match? | ___ | ___ | ___ |

——Yes to all——  No to any  ——Uncertain to any——

Do you know the account number associated with the payment?

Notify the Payment Coordinator to return the check to payer and request a corrected check.

Call Admin. Office at 1-888-555-5555.

No

1. On the Delinquent Payment Menu, click the FIND ACCT tab.
2. Search by typing payer's name, address or telephone number in the appropriate field.
3. Click LOCATE button.

Yes

Did the system locate a matching account number?

Yes  No

1. Write the account number here:
_ _ _ - _ _ _ - _ _.
2. Press F3.

Call Admin. Office at 1-888-555-5555.

1. On the Delinquent Payment Menu, click the PAYMENT tab.
2. In the Open Payment field select the correct account number.
3. Click OK.

*Go to the next page.*

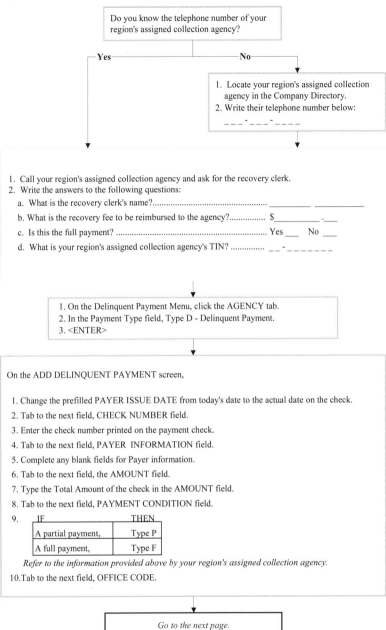

Do you know the telephone number of your region's assigned collection agency?

**Yes** — **No**

1. Locate your region's assigned collection agency in the Company Directory.
2. Write their telephone number below:
   _ _ _ - _ _ _ - _ _ _ _

1. Call your region's assigned collection agency and ask for the recovery clerk.
2. Write the answers to the following questions:
   a. What is the recovery clerk's name?............................................... _____ _____
   b. What is the recovery fee to be reimbursed to the agency?............... $_____ .___
   c. Is this the full payment? ............................................... Yes ___ No ___
   d. What is your region's assigned collection agency's TIN? ............... _ _ - _ _ _ _ _ _ _

1. On the Delinquent Payment Menu, click the AGENCY tab.
2. In the Payment Type field, Type D - Delinquent Payment.
3. <ENTER>

On the ADD DELINQUENT PAYMENT screen,

1. Change the prefilled PAYER ISSUE DATE from today's date to the actual date on the check.

2. Tab to the next field, CHECK NUMBER field.

3. Enter the check number printed on the payment check.

4. Tab to the next field, PAYER INFORMATION field.

5. Complete any blank fields for Payer information.

6. Tab to the next field, the AMOUNT field.

7. Type the Total Amount of the check in the AMOUNT field.

8. Tab to the next field, PAYMENT CONDITION field.

9.
| IF | THEN |
|---|---|
| A partial payment, | Type P |
| A full payment, | Type F |

   *Refer to the information provided above by your region's assigned collection agency.*

10. Tab to the next field, OFFICE CODE.

*Go to the next page.*

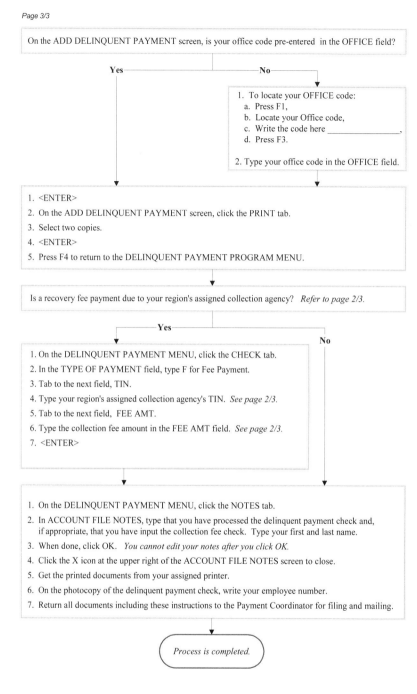

On the ADD DELINQUENT PAYMENT screen, is your office code pre-entered in the OFFICE field?

**Yes** — **No**

1. To locate your OFFICE code:
   a. Press F1,
   b. Locate your Office code,
   c. Write the code here _____,
   d. Press F3.

2. Type your office code in the OFFICE field.

1. \<ENTER>
2. On the ADD DELINQUENT PAYMENT screen, click the PRINT tab.
3. Select two copies.
4. \<ENTER>
5. Press F4 to return to the DELINQUENT PAYMENT PROGRAM MENU.

Is a recovery fee payment due to your region's assigned collection agency? *Refer to page 2/3.*

**Yes** — **No**

1. On the DELINQUENT PAYMENT MENU, click the CHECK tab.
2. In the TYPE OF PAYMENT field, type F for Fee Payment.
3. Tab to the next field, TIN.
4. Type your region's assigned collection agency's TIN. *See page 2/3.*
5. Tab to the next field, FEE AMT.
6. Type the collection fee amount in the FEE AMT field. *See page 2/3.*
7. \<ENTER>

1. On the DELINQUENT PAYMENT MENU, click the NOTES tab.
2. In ACCOUNT FILE NOTES, type that you have processed the delinquent payment check and, if appropriate, that you have input the collection fee check. Type your first and last name.
3. When done, click OK. *You cannot edit your notes after you click OK.*
4. Click the X icon at the upper right of the ACCOUNT FILE NOTES screen to close.
5. Get the printed documents from your assigned printer.
6. On the photocopy of the delinquent payment check, write your employee number.
7. Return all documents including these instructions to the Payment Coordinator for filing and mailing.

*Process is completed.*

# Appendix C: References

# References

Harless, J. H. (1993). *Job aid analysis, design, and development.* Newman, GA: Harless Performance Guild, Inc.

Reynolds, A. (1998, Jan/Feb). Job aids: still a performance support essential. *Technical Training*, Vol. 9, n1: pp. 6–7. ASTD.

Rossett, A. & Gautier-Downes, J. (1991). *A handbook of job aids.* San Diego, CA: Pfeiffer & Company.

San Diego State University (2001). *Job aids.* [Online]. Available: http://edweb.sdsu.edu/courses/edtec540/540www/home.html

Stolovitch, H. D. & Keeps, E. J. (Eds.), Chapter 22, "Job Aids" by Paul H. Elliott (1999), in *Handbook of Human Performance Technology: Improving Individual and Organizational Performance Worldwide* (2nd ed.). San Francisco, CA: Jossey-Bass.

Wynne, J. (2001). *Blast inefficiency with these magic bullets (Part 1).* [Online]. Available: http://www.myplanview.com/expert14.asp

Wynne, J. (2001). *Blast inefficiency with these magic bullets (Part 2).* [Online]. Available: http://www.myplanview.com/expert15.asp

# About the Author

**Charlotte Long, M.S.,** has over 25 years experience in the casualty insurance industry including over 15 years as training manager and practitioner. She also effectively re-organized and maintained the claim procedures for a Fortune 500 company.

She is a Phi Beta Kappa graduate of Pennsylvania State University and has a Masters Degree in Instructional Design from Towson State University. In 2002, she earned the Certificate in Online Instructional Design from Florida State University.

She has numerous professional insurance designations and was recipient of the Society of Insurance Trainers and Educators (SITE) 2003 Innovation Award.

Charlotte Long can be reached at POB 55, Glen Rock PA 17327.

Printed in Canada